Amazing Lifetimes

Written by Keith Pigdon

Series Consultant: Linda Hoyt

T0359793

WorldWise™
Content-based Learning

Contents

Introduction

All living things have a **lifetime**, and some have lifetimes that are amazing.

Some grow very slowly, and some grow very fast. Some have long lifetimes, and others live for a very short time. And during their lifetimes, some living things change in amazing ways. This helps their species survive.

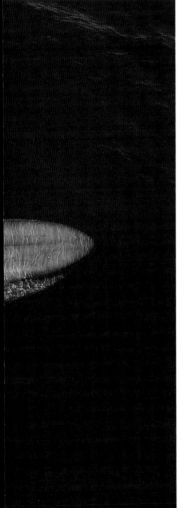
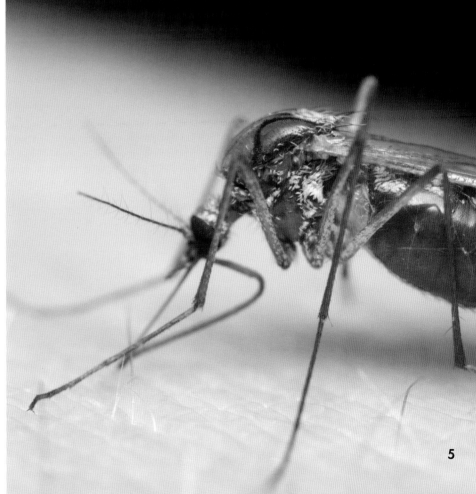

Growing fast

Blue whales grow faster than any other animal.

A blue whale **calf** weighs about two tonnes when it is born – that is as much as the weight of two cars. The calf drinks about 380 litres of its mother's milk every day, and it gets almost four kilograms heavier every hour.

By the time it is seven months old, the calf weighs as much as 20 cars and is about 15 metres long.

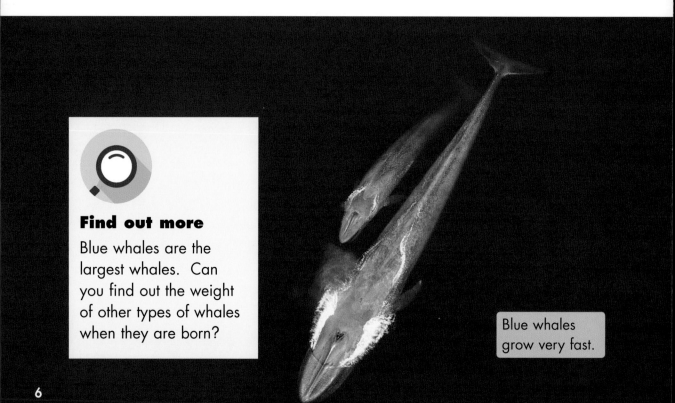

Find out more
Blue whales are the largest whales. Can you find out the weight of other types of whales when they are born?

Blue whales grow very fast.

Bamboo is the fastest-growing plant.

The giant timber bamboo is the fastest-growing bamboo. Some of these young bamboo plants can grow about one metre in 24 hours.

After two months, they can grow to be 18 metres high. That is as tall as a building that is six **storeys** high.

Some bamboo grows very fast.

7

Growing slowly

A plant called the cycad is the slowest-growing plant in the world. Cycad plants look like palm trees, and they grow in places where the weather is warm and wet.

Some cycads are more than 1,000 years old, but only two metres tall. This means that these cycads grow less than two millimetres a year.

Cycads grow very slowly.

Short and long lives

Living for a short time

Some animals have very short **lifetimes**. Many of these animals are insects, such as the mosquito.

The mosquito is very busy during its short lifetime, which lasts for about one week.

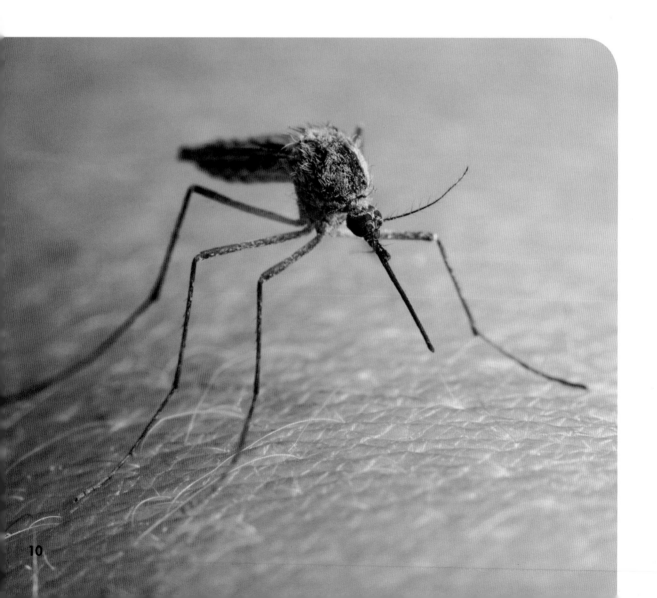

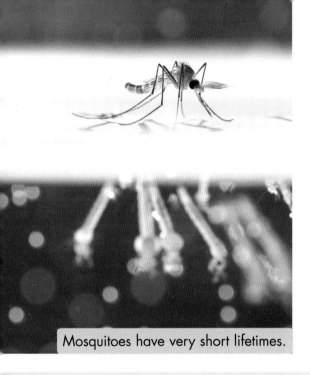
Mosquitoes have very short lifetimes.

Mosquitoes lay their eggs in water. When a mosquito **larva hatches** from its egg, it feeds and grows in the water. The larva changes into a **pupa**. A short time later, an adult mosquito crawls from the pupa. Soon, the adult lays eggs and dies.

All this can happen in one week!

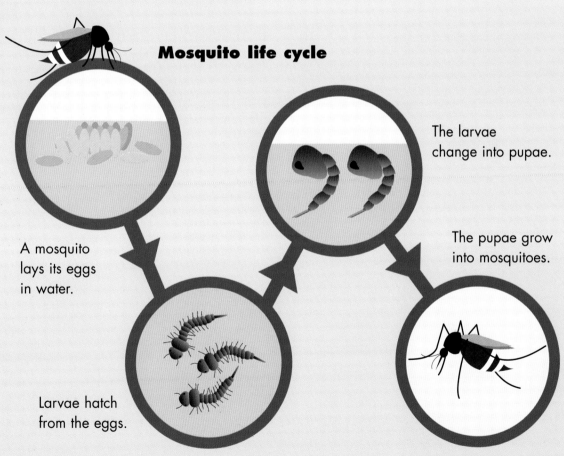

Mosquito life cycle

A mosquito lays its eggs in water.

The larvae change into pupae.

Larvae hatch from the eggs.

The pupae grow into mosquitoes.

Living for a long time

Sea turtles live longer than most other animals in the ocean. They can live for 100 years or more.

Female turtles lay their eggs in sand. When the sand is warm, female babies hatch from the eggs. When the sand is cooler, male babies hatch from the eggs. The baby turtles crawl to the water and swim out to sea.

When they are ready to lay their eggs, female turtles come back to the same place. Some turtles are more than 50 years old when they lay eggs for the first time.

Sea turtles can live for more than 100 years.

Huon pines are one of the oldest living things on Earth.

The Huon pine trees in Tasmania, Australia, are among the oldest living things on Earth. One of these trees has been alive and growing for about 2,000 years.

Huon pines are different from most trees. They grow new trees from the same huge system of underground roots. The trees grow very slowly – between 0.3 and two millimetres per year. They can reach 25 metres in height. Their beautiful timber was once used for building boats. Today, artists make attractive wooden items from Huon pine.

Chapter 3

Changing and returning

An amazing change

A fish called the barramundi has an amazing life.

All barramundi are born as male fish. They live in fresh water for the first three or four years of their lives, then they swim to salty water.

When they are about five years old, the male fish change into female fish.

The female barramundi lay eggs near the **mouth** of a river, and they stay female for the rest of their lives.

During their **lifetime**, barramundi change from male to female.

Find out more

Can you find out about any other animals that change from male to female?

15

Going home to breed

Some salmon **hatch** in streams or rivers. As they grow, they make their way to the ocean.

Before they lay eggs, these salmon find their way back to the stream where they were born. They can swim as far as 3,000 kilometres up rivers, streams and even waterfalls to lay their eggs. The journey can take several months, and the fish do not eat anything once they have left the ocean.

After they have laid their eggs, they die.

Salmon return home to lay their eggs.

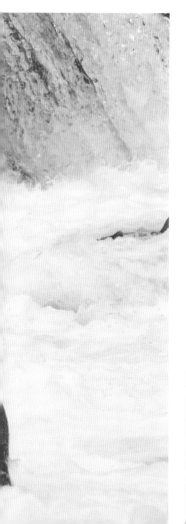

Conclusion

Some plants and animals grow and change in different and surprising ways – some by growing quickly or slowly, others by living for a very short or very long time. Their **lifetimes** are successful because their species continue to live on Earth.

Glossary

calf the young of some large animals such as whales and elephants

hatch to break out of an egg

larva the young of an insect that hatches from eggs and has no wings

lifetime the time that a living thing is alive

mouth the place where a river flows into the ocean

pupa an insect in between the larval stage and adult stage

storeys the different levels of a building

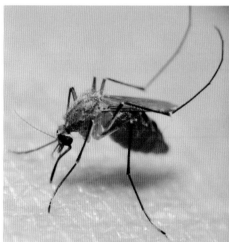

Index

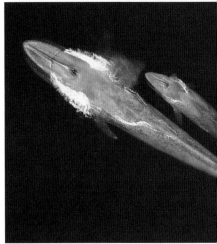